Jungle Tales
Lester's
Adventures

Cover Design By
Lance Raichert

Illustrations By
Ron Coleman

Printed in the United States. All rights reserved.
Copyright 1995

Published by
Pyramid Publishing
P.O. Box 129
Zenda, Wisconsin
53195

Lester was tired of being a lion.

"What kind of animal do you want to be?"
asked his mother.

"I want to be a giraffe," says Lester.

"It's fun being tall."

It's a long way down.

"Maybe it's better to be a hippopotamus."

"Help, I can't breath!"

"Maybe I don't want to be a hippo."

"That looks easy."

"Being a flamingo is boring."

"What a silly way to spend your day."

"Now that looks exciting."

"I'm going to fly."

"Whee, I'm flying."

"I guess I was falling, not flying."

"That looks like fun."

"What do I do now?"

"This is starting to hurt."

"I can help," Lester tells the Elephant.

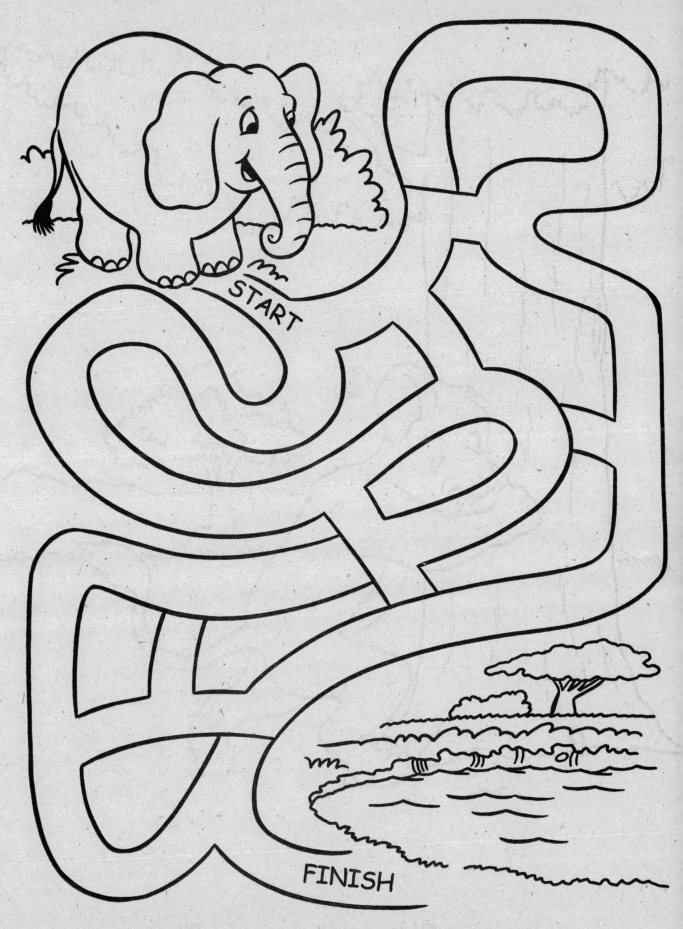

Follow the path to the pond.

"Why isn't it moving?"

"I give up."

Cool water feels good on a hot day.

"Not so hard," pleads Lester.

Time for a swim.

"What's so hard about this?"

"Better close your mouth," the crocodile tells Lester

"Oh no, not this again."

START

FINISH

Lead the cheetah to the plains.

"I'm going to race the cheetah."

"How come he's getting farther ahead?"

"That cheetah is just too fast."

Lester can keep up with the tortoise.

"Wow, this is easy."

"I think I'll be a tortoise."

"Where can I stay dry?" Lester wonders.

"I'm dry in here," the tortoise tells Lester.

"Any room for me?" asks Lester.

"What's down there?" Lester asks the ostrich.

"That hole looks big enough."

"Would somebody please get me out of here?"

"Where is he going in such a hurry?"

"That was fun," the rhinoceros shouts.

START

FINISH

Get the rhino to the tree.

"Here I go."

"Ouch!"

"Now why did I do that?"

"It might be fun to be a snake."

"The sand is scratchy on my stomach."

"At least it didn't hurt my head."

"What are you doing Lester?" asks the hyena.

"I'm trying to be a different animal.
What do hyenas do?"

START

HYENA

FINISH

Show the hyena how to get home.

"We make funny faces."

"I can do that."

"Someday you'll be strong like your father,"
the zebra tells Lester.

"And you will marry a beautiful lioness
like your mother."

"All animals are special, Lester."

"And lions are one of the most special animals of all."

"I'm glad that I'm a lion," Lester tells his parents.

Help Lester find his mother.